#1 FRIEND

FOR THE BEST

FRIEND

EVER

summersdale

FOR THE BEST FRIEND EVER

An Hachette UK Company
www.hachette.co.uk

Summersdale Publishers Ltd
Part of Octopus Publishing Group Limited
Carmelite House
50 Victoria Embankment
LONDON
EC4Y 0DZ

www.summersdale.com

Printed and bound in China

ISBN: 978-1-78685-991-4

Substantial discounts on bulk quantities of Summersdale books are available to corporations, professional associations and other organisations. For details contact general enquiries: telephone: +44 (0) 1243 771107 or email: enquiries@summersdale.com.

TO.. HILDA x .....

FROM.. HILARY ....

SOME PEOPLE GO TO
PRIESTS; OTHERS TO POETRY;
I TO MY FRIENDS.

Virginia Woolf

FRIENDSHIP HAS NO SURVIVAL VALUE; RATHER IT IS ONE OF THOSE THINGS THAT GIVES VALUE TO SURVIVAL.

C. S. Lewis

IT IS ONE OF THE BLESSINGS OF OLD FRIENDS THAT YOU CAN AFFORD TO BE STUPID WITH THEM.

RALPH WALDO EMERSON

HOLD A TRUE FRIEND WITH BOTH YOUR HANDS.

NIGERIAN PROVERB

IF I DON'T HAVE FRIENDS,
THEN I AIN'T GOT NOTHING.

Billie Holiday

WITH MY FRIENDS, I DON'T FEEL PRESSURE TO BE SOMEONE OTHER THAN WHO I AM.

JUDITH GUEST

WHAT IS A FRIEND?
A SINGLE SOUL DWELLING
IN TWO BODIES.

Aristotle

> **FRIENDS, THOSE RELATIONS THAT ONE MAKES FOR ONE'S SELF.**
>
> Eustache Deschamps

YOU'LL

ALWAYS BE

MY FRIEND.

YOU KNOW

TOO MUCH!

THE BEST MIRROR IS
AN OLD FRIEND.

George Herbert

"

MY BEST FRIEND
IS THE MAN WHO
CAN BRING OUT OF
ME MY BEST.

Harris Weinstock

"

THERE IS NOTHING I WOULD NOT DO FOR THOSE WHO ARE REALLY MY FRIENDS.

JANE AUSTEN

FRIENDS ARE THOSE RARE
PEOPLE WHO ASK HOW WE ARE,
AND THEN WAIT TO HEAR
THE ANSWER.

Ed Cunningham

FRIENDS ARE PART OF THE GLUE THAT HOLDS LIFE AND FAITH TOGETHER.

JON KATZ

THE LANGUAGE
OF FRIENDSHIP IS
NOT WORDS BUT
MEANINGS.

HENRY DAVID THOREAU

"

LOTS OF PEOPLE
WANT TO RIDE WITH
YOU IN THE LIMO, BUT
WHAT YOU WANT IS
SOMEONE WHO WILL
TAKE THE BUS WITH
YOU WHEN THE LIMO
BREAKS DOWN.

Oprah Winfrey

"

WHEREVER WE
ARE, IT IS OUR
FRIENDS THAT MAKE
OUR WORLD.

HENRY DRUMMOND

THERE IS NOTHING ON THIS
EARTH MORE TO BE PRIZED
THAN TRUE FRIENDSHIP.

Thomas Aquinas

FOLLOW YOUR
OWN STAR.

Dante Alighieri

I CAN TRUST
MY FRIENDS.
THESE PEOPLE
FORCE ME
TO EXAMINE
MYSELF,
ENCOURAGE
ME TO GROW.

CHER

FRIENDS SHOW THEIR LOVE
IN TIMES OF TROUBLE,
NOT IN HAPPINESS.

Euripides

I'LL ALWAYS

MAKE TIME FOR MY

PARTNER

IN CRIME

THE ONLY WAY TO HAVE A FRIEND IS TO BE ONE.

Ralph Waldo Emerson

YOU HAVE BEEN MY FRIEND...
THAT IN ITSELF IS A
TREMENDOUS THING.

E. B. White

FRIENDSHIP – MY DEFINITION – IS BUILT ON TWO THINGS. RESPECT AND TRUST.

STIEG LARSSON

MY FRIENDS ARE MY ESTATE.

EMILY DICKINSON

A FRIEND
LOVES
AT ALL TIMES.

PROVERBS 17:17

SURROUND YOURSELF WITH PEOPLE WHO ARE THE KETCHUP TO YOUR FRENCH FRIES – THEY MAKE YOU A BETTER VERSION OF YOURSELF.

Grace Helbig

"

TRUE FRIENDSHIP
GIVES NEW LIFE
AND ANIMATION
TO THE OBJECT IT
SUPPORTS.

Robert Burton

A MAN'S FRIENDSHIPS ARE
ONE OF THE BEST MEASURES
OF HIS WORTH.

Charles Darwin

MIX A LITTLE FOOLISHNESS
WITH YOUR SERIOUS PLANS. IT
IS LOVELY TO BE SILLY AT THE
RIGHT MOMENT.

Horace

LOVE LIFE AND LIFE WILL LOVE YOU BACK. LOVE PEOPLE AND THEY WILL LOVE YOU BACK.

ARTHUR RUBINSTEIN

FRIENDS

DON'T LET

FRIENDS FACE

PROBLEMS

ALONE

IN JAIL, A GOOD FRIEND WILL BE TRYING TO BAIL YOU OUT. A BEST FRIEND WILL BE IN THE CELL NEXT TO YOU.

Groucho Marx

YOU'RE BEAUTIFUL AND WORTHY AND TOTALLY UNIQUE.

EMMA STONE

IT'S NOT WHAT WE HAVE,
BUT WHO WE HAVE.

A. A. Milne

OH... THE INEXPRESSIBLE
COMFORT OF FEELING SAFE
WITH A PERSON – HAVING
NEITHER TO WEIGH THOUGHTS
NOR MEASURE WORDS.

Dinah Craik

A SWEET FRIENDSHIP REFRESHES THE SOUL.

PROVERBS 27:9

FRIEND, OUR CLOSENESS IS
THIS: ANYWHERE YOU PUT
YOUR FOOT, FEEL ME IN THE
FIRMNESS UNDER YOU.

Rumi

IF I HAD A FLOWER FOR EVERY TIME I THOUGHT OF YOU... I COULD WALK THROUGH MY GARDEN FOREVER.

ALFRED, LORD TENNYSON

" "

TO LIKE AND TO
DISLIKE THE SAME
THINGS, THIS
IS INDEED TRUE
FRIENDSHIP.

Sallust

" "

EACH FRIEND REPRESENTS A WORLD IN US, A WORLD POSSIBLY NOT BORN UNTIL THEY ARRIVE, AND IT IS ONLY BY THIS MEETING THAT A NEW WORLD IS BORN.

ANAÏS NIN

'TIS THE PRIVILEGE
OF FRIENDSHIP TO
TALK NONSENSE,
AND TO HAVE
THIS NONSENSE
RESPECTED.

CHARLES LAMB

FRIENDSHIPS ARE DISCOVERED, RATHER THAN MADE.

Harriet Beecher Stowe

"

NOTHING MAKES
THE EARTH SEEM
SO SPACIOUS AS TO
HAVE FRIENDS AT
A DISTANCE; THEY
MAKE THE LATITUDES
AND LONGITUDES.

Henry David Thoreau

"

THE MOST BEAUTIFUL
DISCOVERY TRUE FRIENDS
MAKE IS THAT THEY CAN
GROW SEPARATELY WITHOUT
GROWING APART.

Elizabeth Foley

THERE'S NOTHING LIKE A
REALLY LOYAL, DEPENDABLE,
GOOD FRIEND. NOTHING.

Jennifer Aniston

WE ARE MY

FAVOURITE

DOUBLE ACT

WISHING TO BE FRIENDS IS QUICK WORK, BUT FRIENDSHIP IS A SLOW RIPENING FRUIT.

ARISTOTLE

CLOSE FRIENDS ARE TRULY LIFE'S TREASURES. SOMETIMES THEY KNOW US BETTER THAN WE KNOW OURSELVES.

Vincent van Gogh

A TRUE FRIEND
IS SOMEONE
WHO THINKS
THAT YOU ARE
A GOOD EGG
EVEN THOUGH
HE KNOWS
THAT YOU
ARE SLIGHTLY
CRACKED.

BERNARD MELTZER

WHAT IS A FRIEND? I WILL TELL YOU. IT IS A PERSON WITH WHOM YOU DARE TO BE YOURSELF.

FRANK CRANE

TRUE FRIENDS ARE LIKE
DIAMONDS — BRIGHT,
BEAUTIFUL, VALUABLE,
AND ALWAYS IN STYLE.

Nicole Richie

LET THERE BE NO PURPOSE
IN FRIENDSHIP SAVE THE
DEEPENING OF THE SPIRIT.

Khalil Gibran

LOVE IS NOT
CONSOLATION.
IT IS LIGHT.

Friedrich Nietzsche

ONE OF THE
MOST BEAUTIFUL
QUALITIES OF TRUE
FRIENDSHIP IS TO
UNDERSTAND AND TO
BE UNDERSTOOD.

SENECA THE YOUNGER

FRIENDS ARE THE
SUNSHINE OF LIFE.

John Hay

I COUNT MYSELF IN NOTHING ELSE SO HAPPY, AS IN A SOUL REMEMBERING MY GOOD FRIENDS.

William Shakespeare

BE SLOW IN CHOOSING A FRIEND, SLOWER IN CHANGING.

BENJAMIN FRANKLIN

WE MET
BY CHANCE
BUT BECAME
FRIENDS
BY CHOICE

"

ONE OF THE SECRETS OF LIFE IS THAT ALL THAT IS REALLY WORTH THE DOING IS WHAT WE DO FOR OTHERS.

Lewis Carroll

LET US
BE GRATEFUL TO
PEOPLE WHO MAKE
US HAPPY; THEY
ARE THE CHARMING
GARDENERS WHO
MAKE OUR SOULS
BLOSSOM.

MARCEL PROUST

MY DEFINITION OF A FRIEND
IS SOMEBODY WHO ADORES
YOU, EVEN THOUGH THEY
KNOW THE THINGS YOU'RE
MOST ASHAMED OF.

Jodie Foster

YOUR FRIEND IS THE MAN WHO KNOWS ALL ABOUT YOU, AND STILL LOVES YOU.

ELBERT HUBBARD

TO BE RICH IN FRIENDS IS
TO BE POOR IN NOTHING.

Lilian Whiting

DO YOUR THING
AND DON'T CARE IF THEY LIKE IT.

TINA FEY

A FRIEND IS ONE WHO
OVERLOOKS YOUR BROKEN
FENCE AND ADMIRES THE
FLOWERS IN YOUR GARDEN.

Anonymous

FRIENDSHIP MARKS A LIFE EVEN MORE DEEPLY THAN LOVE. LOVE RISKS DEGENERATING INTO OBSESSION, FRIENDSHIP IS NEVER ANYTHING BUT SHARING.

Elie Wiesel

A TRUE FRIEND IS SOMEONE WHO IS THERE FOR YOU WHEN HE'D RATHER BE ANYWHERE ELSE.

LEN WEIN

FIND A GROUP OF PEOPLE WHO CHALLENGE AND INSPIRE YOU; SPEND A LOT OF TIME WITH THEM, AND IT WILL CHANGE YOUR LIFE.

Amy Poehler

FRIENDSHIP IS A WILDLY UNDERRATED MEDICATION.

Anna Deavere Smith

ALL LOVE THAT
HAS NOT FRIENDSHIP
FOR ITS BASE, IS LIKE
A MANSION BUILT
UPON THE SAND.

ELLA WHEELER WILCOX

THE MOST PRECIOUS OF ALL
POSSESSIONS IS A WISE
AND LOYAL FRIEND.

Herodotus

IT IS A SWEET THING, FRIENDSHIP, A DEAR BALM, A HAPPY AND AUSPICIOUS BIRD OF CALM.

PERCY BYSSHE SHELLEY

FRIENDSHIP IS THE SOURCE OF
THE GREATEST PLEASURES, AND
WITHOUT FRIENDS EVEN THE
MOST AGREEABLE PURSUITS
BECOME TEDIOUS.

Thomas Aquinas

"

THINGS ARE NEVER
QUITE AS SCARY
WHEN YOU'VE GOT
A BEST FRIEND.

Bill Watterson

"

I HAVE FRIENDS
IN OVERALLS
WHOSE
FRIENDSHIP I
WOULD NOT
SWAP FOR THE
FAVOUR OF
THE KINGS OF
THE WORLD.

THOMAS EDISON

A MAN...
SHOULD KEEP
HIS FRIENDSHIP
IN CONSTANT
REPAIR.

SAMUEL JOHNSON

THE REAL TEST OF FRIENDSHIP IS:
CAN YOU LITERALLY DO NOTHING
WITH THE OTHER PERSON? CAN
YOU ENJOY THOSE MOMENTS OF
LIFE THAT ARE UTTERLY SIMPLE?

Eugene Kennedy

NEVER DOUBT
THAT YOU ARE
VALUABLE AND
POWERFUL AND
DESERVING OF
EVERY CHANCE AND
OPPORTUNITY IN
THE WORLD.

HILLARY CLINTON

THE ROAD TO A FRIEND'S
HOUSE IS NEVER LONG.

Danish proverb

ANY DAY SPENT WITH YOU IS MY FAVOURITE DAY. SO TODAY IS MY NEW FAVOURITE DAY.

A. A. Milne

FRIENDSHIP IS A STRONG AND HABITUAL INCLINATION IN TWO PERSONS TO PROMOTE THE GOOD AND HAPPINESS OF ONE ANOTHER.

EUSTACE BUDGELL

THE BIRD A NEST,
THE SPIDER A WEB,
MAN FRIENDSHIP.

William Blake

A GOOD FRIEND

KNOWS YOUR STORIES,
BUT A TRUE

FRIEND

HELPED YOU
WRITE THEM

JUST BE YOURSELF,
THERE IS NO ONE BETTER.

Taylor Swift

RARE AS
IS TRUE LOVE,
TRUE
FRIENDSHIP
IS RARER.

JEAN DE LA FONTAINE

IT'S NOT THAT DIAMONDS ARE A GIRL'S BEST FRIEND, BUT IT'S YOUR BEST FRIENDS WHO ARE YOUR DIAMONDS.

Gina Barreca

WHEREVER YOU GO, GO WITH ALL YOUR HEART.

CONFUCIUS

WE ARE ALL TRAVELLERS IN THE
WILDERNESS OF THIS WORLD, AND
THE BEST WE CAN FIND IN OUR
TRAVELS IS AN HONEST FRIEND.

Robert Louis Stevenson

> **ONE LOYAL FRIEND IS WORTH TEN THOUSAND RELATIVES.**
>
> Euripides

IT TAKES A LONG TIME TO GROW AN OLD FRIEND.

JOHN LEONARD

GROWING APART DOESN'T
CHANGE THE FACT THAT FOR A
LONG TIME WE GREW SIDE BY
SIDE; OUR ROOTS WILL ALWAYS
BE TANGLED. I'M GLAD FOR THAT.

Ally Condie

TALK NOT OF WASTED AFFECTION: AFFECTION NEVER WAS WASTED.

HENRY WADSWORTH LONGFELLOW

FRIENDSHIP CONSISTS IN
FORGETTING WHAT ONE GIVES,
AND REMEMBERING WHAT
ONE RECEIVES.

Alexander Dumas

IF YOU HAVE NOTHING IN
LIFE BUT A GOOD FRIEND,
YOU'RE RICH.

Michelle Kwan

A FRIENDSHIP THAT CAN END NEVER REALLY BEGAN.

Publilius Syrus

DON'T WALK
BEHIND ME; I MAY
NOT LEAD. DON'T
WALK IN FRONT
OF ME; I MAY NOT
FOLLOW. JUST WALK
BESIDE ME AND
BE MY FRIEND.

ALBERT CAMUS

FRIENDSHIP IS A PROMISE, NOT A LABEL

SINCE THERE IS NOTHING SO WELL WORTH HAVING AS FRIENDS, NEVER LOSE A CHANCE TO MAKE THEM.

FRANCESCO GUICCIARDINI

THEY MAKE ME
STRONGER;
THEY MAKE ME
BRAVER.

JANE FONDA ON HER FRIENDS

IT'S THE FRIENDS
YOU CAN CALL UP AT
4 A.M. THAT MATTER.

Marlene Dietrich

> "FRIENDSHIP IMPROVES HAPPINESS, AND ABATES MISERY, BY THE DOUBLING OF OUR JOY AND THE DIVIDING OF OUR GRIEF."
>
> Marcus Tullius Cicero

IN THE SWEETNESS OF FRIENDSHIP
LET THERE BE LAUGHTER,
AND SHARING OF PLEASURES.
FOR IN THE DEW OF LITTLE
THINGS THE HEART FINDS ITS
MORNING AND IS REFRESHED.

Khalil Gibran

FRIENDSHIP IS BORN AT THE
MOMENT ONE PERSON SAYS TO
ANOTHER, 'WHAT? YOU TOO? I
THOUGHT I WAS THE ONLY ONE.'

C. S. Lewis

TIME DOESN'T TAKE AWAY FROM FRIENDSHIP, NOR DOES SEPARATION.

TENNESSEE WILLIAMS

A GOOD FRIEND IS A
CONNECTION TO LIFE — A TIE
TO THE PAST, A ROAD TO THE
FUTURE, THE KEY TO SANITY IN
A TOTALLY INSANE WORLD.

Lois Wyse

"

A SINGLE ROSE
CAN BE MY GARDEN;
A SINGLE FRIEND,
MY WORLD.

Leo Buscaglia

"

ONE FRIEND

CAN CHANGE
YOUR WHOLE
 LIFE

A FRIEND MAY BE
WAITING BEHIND A
STRANGER'S FACE.

MAYA ANGELOU

BE SLOW TO FALL INTO
FRIENDSHIP, BUT WHEN
YOU ARE IN, CONTINUE
FIRM AND CONSTANT.

Socrates

THE GREATEST GIFT OF LIFE IS FRIENDSHIP, AND I HAVE RECEIVED IT.

HUBERT H. HUMPHREY

WE ARE LIKE
ISLANDS IN THE
SEA, SEPARATE ON
THE SURFACE BUT
CONNECTED
IN THE DEEP.

WILLIAM JAMES

SILENCE

MAKE THE REAL
CONVERSATIONS
BETWEEN FRIENDS.
NOT THE SAYING,
BUT THE NEVER
NEEDING TO SAY
THAT COUNTS.

Margaret Lee Runbeck

TO LOVE AND BE LOVED IS TO FEEL THE SUN FROM BOTH SIDES.

DAVID VISCOTT

A TRUE FRIEND IS SOMEONE
WHO LETS YOU HAVE TOTAL
FREEDOM TO BE YOURSELF.

Jim Morrison

LONGEVITY IS SOMETHING YOU REALLY CAN FIND VERY PRECIOUS AND RARE IN FRIENDSHIPS.

Taylor Swift

A FRIEND MAY WELL BE
RECKONED THE MASTERPIECE
OF NATURE.

Ralph Waldo Emerson

FRIENDSHIP IS THE PUREST LOVE.

OSHO

"

BE
UNAPOLOGETICALLY
YOU.

Steve Maraboli

"

THE SINCERE FRIENDS OF THIS WORLD ARE AS SHIP LIGHTS IN THE STORMIEST OF NIGHTS.

GIOTTO DI BONDONE

A TRUE FRIEND IS SOMEONE
WHO IS ALWAYS THERE DURING
THE UPS AND DOWNS.

Miley Cyrus

FRIENDSHIP

IS A KNOT

THAT CANNOT

BE UNTIED

WITHOUT FRIENDS, NO ONE WOULD WANT TO LIVE, EVEN IF HE HAD ALL OTHER GOODS.

ARISTOTLE

I THINK ABOUT MY BEST FRIENDSHIP… AS LIKE A GREAT ROMANCE OF MY YOUNG LIFE.

Lena Dunham

A GOOD FRIEND IS CHEAPER THAN THERAPY.

Anonymous

LIFE IS PARTLY WHAT WE MAKE IT, AND PARTLY WHAT IT IS MADE BY THE FRIENDS WE CHOOSE.

TEHYI HSIEH

ANYTHING IS POSSIBLE WHEN
YOU HAVE THE RIGHT PEOPLE
THERE TO SUPPORT YOU.

Misty Copeland

"

TRY TO BE A
RAINBOW IN
SOMEONE'S
CLOUD.

Maya Angelou

"

FRIENDSHIP IS PRECIOUS, NOT
ONLY IN THE SHADE, BUT IN
THE SUNSHINE OF LIFE.

Thomas Jefferson

THE HEART
THAT LOVES IS
ALWAYS YOUNG.

GREEK PROVERB

THE IDEAL FRIENDSHIP IS TO FEEL AS ONE WHILE REMAINING TWO.

SOPHIE SWETCHINE

IF WE TREATED OURSELVES AS WELL AS WE TREATED OUR BEST FRIEND, CAN YOU IMAGINE?

MEGHAN, DUCHESS OF SUSSEX

BE YOURSELF. DO WHATEVER
YOU WANT TO DO AND DON'T LET
BOUNDARIES HOLD YOU BACK.

Sophie Turner

" "

IF YOU GO LOOKING
FOR A FRIEND,
YOU'RE GOING TO
FIND THEY'RE VERY
SCARCE. IF YOU GO
OUT TO BE A FRIEND,
YOU'LL FIND THEM
EVERYWHERE.

Zig Ziglar

" "

SOMEONE TO TELL IT TO IS
ONE OF THE FUNDAMENTAL
NEEDS OF HUMAN BEINGS.

Miles Franklin

I MAY NOT

ALWAYS BE THERE
WITH YOU,
BUT I WILL
ALWAYS BE THERE

FOR YOU

NO FRIENDSHIP IS AN ACCIDENT.

O. HENRY

THEY MAY FORGET WHAT
YOU SAID, BUT THEY WILL
NEVER FORGET HOW YOU
MADE THEM FEEL.

Carl W. Buechner

"

IF YOU REMEMBER
ME, THEN I DON'T
CARE IF EVERYONE
ELSE FORGETS.

Haruki Murakami

"

FRIENDSHIP IS THE ONLY... GUARANTEE OF PEACE.

BUDDHA

A FRIEND IS WHAT THE HEART
NEEDS ALL THE TIME.

Henry Van Dyke

If you're interested in finding out more about our books, find us on Facebook at **Summersdale Publishers** and follow us on Twitter at **@Summersdale**.

www.summersdale.com

Image credits

'STAY' IS A CHARMING WORD IN A FRIEND'S VOCABULARY.

AMOS BRONSON ALCOTT

WE'LL BE FRIENDS UNTIL
WE'RE OLD AND SENILE... THEN
WE'LL BE NEW FRIENDS!

Anonymous

I LEARNED THAT A
REAL FRIENDSHIP
IS NOT ABOUT WHAT
YOU CAN GET, BUT
WHAT YOU CAN GIVE.

ERIC THOMAS

NO ROAD IS LONG WITH GOOD COMPANY.

Turkish proverb

"

THE FINEST KIND
OF FRIENDSHIP IS
BETWEEN PEOPLE
WHO EXPECT A GREAT
DEAL OF EACH OTHER
BUT NEVER ASK IT.

Sylvia Bremer

"

SOME FRIENDS PLAY AT FRIENDSHIP BUT A TRUE FRIEND STICKS CLOSER THAN ONE'S NEAREST KIN.

PROVERBS 18:24

LIFE IS TO BE FORTIFIED
BY MANY FRIENDSHIPS. TO
LOVE, AND TO BE LOVED, IS
THE GREATEST HAPPINESS
OF EXISTENCE.

Sydney Smith

FRIENDSHIP IS THE ONLY CEMENT THAT WILL EVER HOLD THE WORLD TOGETHER.

Woodrow Wilson

1 PLANET,

7 CONTINENTS,

HUNDREDS OF

COUNTRIES...

AND I HAD THE

PRIVILEGE OF

MEETING YOU

FRIENDSHIP IS
THE MARRIAGE
OF AFFECTIONS.

Thomas Watson

FRIENDSHIP IS A SHELTERING TREE.

SAMUEL TAYLOR COLERIDGE

SURROUND YOURSELF
WITH ONLY PEOPLE
WHO ARE GOING TO
LIFT YOU HIGHER.

OPRAH WINFREY

TRUE FRIENDS ARE FAMILIES WHICH YOU CAN SELECT.

Audrey Hepburn

DON'T ALLOW THE GRASS TO GROW ON THE PATH OF FRIENDSHIP.

NATIVE AMERICAN PROVERB